To : Lynda
With love from

OCTOBER 2008 ✓

UNDRESSING IN WINTER

BY THE SAME AUTHOR

Poetry

Performances

Plays

Blighty
In the Shadows
A Secret Passion
Entirely Ethel
Intimacies
Twockers, Knockers and Elsie Smith
Journey

Jean Stevens

UNDRESSING IN WINTER

Matador
9 De Montfort Mews
Leicester LE1 7FW, UK
Tel: (+44) 116 255 9311 / 9312
Email: books@troubador.co.uk
Web: www.troubador.co.uk/matador

ISBN 978 1906510 657

Typeset in 12pt Bembo by Troubador Publishing Ltd, Leicester, UK

Matador is an imprint of Troubador Publishing Ltd

Contents

Acknowledgements	7
His Clothes	11
An Avenue of Silver Mercs	12
Singing the World	13
Picnic at Hanging Rock	14
The Red Centre – Uluru	15
Her Glass	16
Shelved	17
Walking in Derbyshire	18
Wrapped in Tissue Paper	19
Undressing in Winter	20
The Portmanteau of Dreams	21
Road Accident	22
Poppies	23
Stainforth Force	24
Stubborn Memory	26
Workman Cleaning a Statue	27
Masks	28
A Small Silence	29
A Few More Adjustments	30
With Every New Game	31
Haunting	32
In the Blood	33
Domination of White	34

Derelict   35

Sunlight has Tricked the Garden   36

Museum   37

Post-War Game   39

Visit to the Psychiatric Unit   40

Repairs   41

Your Smile   42

Jacket   43

Small Boy in Irons   44

Let's Face It   45

The Magical Mundane   46

Fire and Ice in Cambridge   48

When the Time has Come   49

Burned   51

White Ovver   52

To a Friend Losing Her Sight   53

Literary Weekend   54

Pistol   55

Love Poem – a Prisoner's Request   56

How Far Will You Go?   57

Inside   58

For My Today Girls of Tomorrow   59

Acknowledgements

Arvon Press Anthology, Bananas, Expression One, The Honest Ulsterman, Iron, The Little Word Machine, Meridian, New Poetry 3 (Arts Council Anthology), New Poetry (Radio 4), Northern Drift (Radio 3), Oasis, Outposts, P.E.N. New Poems Anthology, Pennine Platform, Poetry and Audience, Poets are People (B.B.C.Radio), Samphire, Transcript, Words, and *The Yorkshire Post.*

UNDRESSING
IN WINTER

His Clothes

She asked me to sort through his clothes.
I stood by the bed they shared for fifty years,
finally made myself open cupboards,
pile up his life on the patchwork quilt:
the new suit he bought – and wore just once;
the shirts not only ironed but starched;
the worn vests and pants. Intrusive,
to fold and pack my father's underwear.

The Sally Army wanted pockets empty.
Trousers, jackets, coats were vague and vacant.
I held on, thought of nothing, anything,
and almost made it to the end.

Then I held his driving licence – solid, dated, named.
The room whirled, the years peeled back. I was undone.

An Avenue of Silver Mercs

I walked the avenue of affluent houses,
manicured gardens, spotless paths,
and Merc after Merc, neatly parked.

These people were sophisticated, smart;
these people had got it sussed.

The opposite of me. I'm crumbly, messy, uncontained.
I felt those svelte and opulent cars
silently whisper messages of contempt.

It was like when you trail along the winter streets
and house after house reverberates with light,
each room a stage-set of layered velvets,
deep in burgundies and gold. Safe and sorted.
And you're outside. Wet, dishevelled, and falling apart.

A lone dog barked. A door slammed.
Our worlds became one:
the place where everyone strives
to hold back the creeping cold.

You in your silver cars
and me in my Oxfam scarf.

Singing the World

Walking the world with his song
the Aboriginal creates himself.

Now I sing my name, Gift of God,
gift of the god that is man.

I would like to name deserts, oases,
the watering places of the world;

to sing the blue haze of the eucalypt,
the perfumed splendour of the tree.

I would like to spring from mud,
the same mud that formed the kangaroo.

As I rise, all I can name as totems,
drawn each morning from earth's crust,

are my marriage bed, cradle and coffin,
the cool white touch of linen,

the tamed water of my shower,
miles from wells and springs and creeks.

But here also are hard and barren places
which may lead to the gathered light.

Is this enough? Can I go walkabout in my own land,
dare to step forward and sing?

I must place footprint after footprint
and create my life.

Picnic at Hanging Rock

It's a glorious day
and we, too, are having a picnic.
Right here, where the girls disappeared.

In the burning light,
I touch the hot implacability of Hanging Rock,
imagine them easing into sexual maturity,
blending with nature,
ghosting into parallel lives –
or whatever explanation suits the times.

That day in nineteen-hundred their watches stopped.
Our watches move inexorably
but why has the camera jammed?

Of course, these girls did not disappear
for they never existed.
Yet actually they do exist
more than if they *had* existed
because they're here now
trying to teach me something.

And this isn't a *glorious day*
meaning only the sun's bright touch.
It's a day full of glory.

But I've had too much maturity of every kind
and can't quite slip into knowledge.
They're holding out their hands,
telling me the hidden painted cave holds what I need –
and still the Rock won't take me.

I'm a stubborn pupil
and have much to unlearn.

The Red Centre – Uluru

Partway up Ayers Rock, trapped by the killer wind,
I hang, bruised, over the hot, hypnotic chasm.
Dozens have been hooked by death right here.
Why should the Spirits of this place save me,
a white and anally-retentive Pom
who knowingly breaks taboos?

Breathe, claw, breathe, claw, breathe.
Bleeding from knees, hands, nails, now I'm *singing*.
A psalm, a hymn, a song of Alcheringa the mystic Dreamtime?
No, I'm singing *The tide is high but I'm holding on*.

Limbs frenetic, lungs flailing, I reach the top.
Already there, my daughter cheers.
A Chinese woman, an Australian man,
and a Japanese camera embrace me.

Something at the centre of me gives.
Something in me receives.
Suddenly, I start to take myself seriously.

Her Glass

Her glass showed her she was plain.
This knowledge shadowed all she did,
followed her through her days, her dreams,
the stranglehold that held her gasping;
plunged her into the dark, kept her there,
away from seas, valleys, woodlands, mountains,
away from the world. Away from light.

But light came looking for her. She was needed
in a country broken by war and waste.
The skills she had learned as substitutes
made plain the grief of shadowy strangers.
Now she does not look into the glass
but through the glass to other lives
and in dark gutters finds her mountains.

Shelved

He lives in manageable yesterdays
for today has robbed him of tomorrow.

Seven-league boots were once not big enough
for one who now can spread his toes only
as far as the worn boundaries of dead
domestic fur. His heroes, those Tarzans
of ungovernable forests, have shrunk,
like his outlook, cramped by the tiny frame
near which only his body seems to sit.

His fretting for substance has undressed
more and more of the bone and yet, within
that skeleton, journeys of the blood remain.
But horizons may prove as fictional
as heroes and, while the boxed future fades
to the last dot of light, he has to wait
for officials to direct his life.

And it was the authorised who mugged him
through two world wars and the night shifts of peace.

Walking in Derbyshire

She had to wear her red bobble hat
because of the rain and fierce cold.
A clenched jaw set her face in stone.
For months she'd refused hats or scarves
and wore her hairless head with defiance.
Now this lack of choice made her
scythe through Eyam, Stoney Middleton,
Speedwell, for two whole days,
a woman stamping the devil out of nature.

I naïvely imagined we'd talk about *things*
look for some brightness to clutch
but could have more easily demolished
every drystone wall in the county
and transported the debris to hell
than have dared to form a relevant word.

Our weekend over, we went back to the car
as the weather turned around
and the sun struck the windscreen
in malevolent flashes of light.

We set our faces towards home,
still stony, unable to cross
the chasm we had dug.

The last we saw of the village
was a simple road sign:
Thank you for driving safely through Hope.

Wrapped in Tissue Paper

Now, she wears her new scarlet sweater,
the snuggly collar draped at the neck,
gazes with joy at the tattered tree
dragged down by her Dad from the dusty loft,
touches the magic of blue icicles, gold stars,
white angels and the three wise men in purple
her Mum takes out of tissue every year.

Tonight, aunts, uncles, cousins will arrive,
stamp snow off their shoes, steam the air
with their breath. All will have walked.
None is rich enough to own a car.
It's a ritual. Her house Christmas Eve,
Aunt Evelyn Boxing Day, cousin Ken on New Year's Eve.
This is the delicious moment of anticipation.

Later, she will lie in bed warmed by the low
scribble of adult voices downstairs. Friends will call
and whisper about presents brought for her.
She doesn't believe in Father Christmas –
not since she was three – but still hangs up
a pillow case, puts sherry by the hearth.

Today, that girl is a ghost
in the haloed light at the diminishing end
of a long dark tunnel; and that time,
that place, are now an unreachable world.

Undressing in Winter

I pause by the ruined barn where far hills rise
jagged against the sky and seem within reach
of my fingers. Winter likes clarity and dares
to strip away the frippery of leaves, the accessories
of blossom, to expose tough sinews of branch and twig,
shrivelled brown stalks, and the origin of things,

like a woman who throws aside her lipstick
and her comb and stares clear-eyed into the glass.
A chaffinch is etched against the blue, his throat trembling
with song, a rabbit hurls itself across the raked field
while, distant and sharp in the quiet cold, a dog barks,
and I almost feel ready to say *yes* to this naked dare.

I turn for home. The bite of rocks under my feet
goes to the bone, mud tangles trousers and boots;
but look, moments before the dark, the sky blooms
turquoise, pink, purple, as the last of the sun,
a red curve behind the horizon, cuts through
the cloud in streams of apocalyptic light.

The Portmanteau of Dreams

In my portmanteau, I will pack
Mosi-oa-Tunya the Smoke that Thunders,
meltings of chocolate on my tongue,
my father singing *I'll Walk Beside You*,
and the scent of log-burning fires.

My case will be made from a silken shawl,
tougher than any armoured box,
and will trail its golden fringes,
carelessly knotted and wild.

I will float my portmanteau in the sky
with no ropes, no locks, no chains,
among swooping, dangerous birds.

Road Accident

You were carried home mottled in blood
and dirt. Dark blue uniforms crowded
round you frozen in marble childhood.

My senses, dodging pain, focussed on the wail
of sirens, fingers on a steering wheel,
and the ricochet of nightmare speed.

I watched as you were rushed inside the place
you saw as having windows but no light
and wondered if all gestures come too late.

But there, under trained hands, machines were
allies and, when I learned you would recover,
my assumed control began to waver.

Bear-like, I hugged you with instinctive
force, making you cry out and me believe
the animal ferocity of love.

Poppies

The Flanders poppy speaks of trenches,
mud and wasteland. Its strength lies
in a paper delicacy of unmistakeable red,
and its stubborn place within cornfields.

In the garden, a voluptuous cousin sprawls,
drawing attention like a stripper who slowly
uncurls each layer of blowsy scarlet
to reveal the dark heart of harvest.

Both poppies hold fast to the gritty
patience of earth. They will continue
to scatter seed and push their way into life
through whatever has smothered them.

However many ages dormant or trampled down,
they will come back, be here long after men
have sunk and rotted beneath the soil,
never to set seed, never to rise again.

Stainforth Force

The salmon are running
hour after hour they leap up
the falls and are battered back
pink and silver arcs crossing
the refracted gold of winter sun
against the force of plunging water

They have battled tides wind
hunger from Icelandic waters
through the breaking North Atlantic
to switchback the cold waves
between Ireland's ephemeral green
and the purple heath of Scotland

day after night after day of miles
always fighting the wilful current
to the spilling mouth of the Ribble
itself impelled by nature
to race for ever seaward
with the ice-melt of the years

They must evade the keen beaks
of heron and reverse history
swimming ever upwards and back
to their high spawning ground
among limestone and millstone grit
in the glacial Yorkshire Dales

I ask whatever gods may be
that I might share this splendour
one more year two three ten

witness the stubbornness of life
to leap curve sparkle fight
through all the trials set by chance
and take hold of the courage to make
my own defiant silver arc
against the darkening day

Stubborn Memory

Grey council officials moved him out,
this man who laboured, paid his bills, and volunteered.

And year upon year after his death
I still can't crush the picture in my head:

They packed wedding albums, baby shawls, retirement clocks,
and now he stooped in their long-tended garden.

My father's hands were red with blood.
Bent against the rain, he was digging up his roses.

Workman Cleaning a Statue

The Black Prince, his horse's red fuel frozen,
perpetually rides down City Square,
tilting towards who knows what destination
and, fixed, can never turn to see behind him

that curiously less alive church garden
where, gripped by creeping weeds, the soil sickens.
And touching all, constant in its blackening work,
the necessary air erodes both flesh and bronze.

Blue denim hiding his decay, the workman
scrubs a century's stale breath, his fingers cautious,
as if what many generations darkened,
rising again, might gallop under his hands.

Masks

Are the masks grotesque your side?
From here they now seem normal.
Safe inside elastic skin,
clown's the one I most parade –
flashing its perpetual
manufactured grin – but can

plaster on a sapient
front if the company is
scholarly. When I'm weary
after nights of weeping, paint
on lips and cheeks, dark glasses,
making up a forgery,

depict a woman at peace,
but behind the bars that lock
my eyes a hooligan stirs
Saturdays on the terrace.
Performing on a public
stage I once agreed to strip.

Each rehearsed betraying dance
unwound to anti-climax:
flesh reveals nothing at all.
And there's not an audience
in the world for whom I'd take
off this bright and stilted smile.

A Small Silence

A small silence among so many,
one private minus in death's immense
front-page arithmetic, for earth
accommodates too well the whitening
evidence of those who did not choose.

You let light into your own wound-up days,
shadowed the faced future for others
who keep the imprint of your going
and outwardly place among numerous
columns your individual stone.

A Few More Adjustments

Too big, the picture spilled vistas
far beyond the frame. Frustrating,
because that oak, inherited
from my mother's mother, stands solid
as coffin sides, more rigid
than modern margins.

Cutting canvas to fit was challenging.
The angel fell first, then the man
in shining armour, and the tree's topmost
reach. A knife slip turned the child's
smile to idiot grin but, centrally,
the madonna remained unchanged.

A few more adjustments crammed
the figures within right angles,
although creases impaired the sun
and the chair had crippled legs.
Now the whole painting's begun to crack
but the frame's intact.

With Every New Game

With every new game
the odds remain immovably the same.

Widening dimensions intensify the fight;
but kings remain strictly black or white.

Allied to the white persuasion,
I lack self-denial, choose evasion

and, fearing crucial moves, wait
once more to blunder into checkmate.

Shah mata – the king is dead; long live the king.
The black antagonist moving

ahead asserts his phoenix
promise of more expedient kicks.

Show me a coward's compromise,
a grey monarch resurrecting old lies.

A reconciliation would dispense
with the trial. Too weary for defence

I lie with the discarded weak
but it isn't justice that I seek.

Haunting

We took possession of this house
and all its keys, but there's one key
for which we never found a lock,
although there are seven locks at least,
and none keeps out the prowling wind.
If the original owner came back
could he provide an answer?

Perhaps it could be melted down
to make a coin or a knife-blade,
something useful. Hanging redundant
on a rusty nail it seems to accuse,
the ghost of a ghost without a place
to haunt or guarantee of second
death to obliterate the first.

It's like being given the password
for a far and sinless city
you can never hope to reach;
whereas a keyless lock provides
a simple problem that might be solved
with ease by any locksmith –
or any burglar, come to that.

In the Blood

She mended her days, patching poverty while
the slump dragged on, yet she left no sordid
memory to corrupt when mangle, black-lead,
broom and cradle remained idle

reminders of drudgery camouflaged
by dignity, although more than cancer
devoured her. Slowly my father's mother
died. At ten he knew enough to hide smudged

eyes, wept in bed when the widower's snores
mocked the dark. She did not sleep. She came back
and, with words her only material, spoke
the boy's name, and what she repaired endures.

My maternal grandmother abandoned
dolls when eight, forced to act midwife
to her own mother, flushing that drained life
from slop bucket to privy. Then she buried

her toys, was imprisoned by sink, flat-iron,
the rickets of real babies, and broken
nights fighting mucus as diphtheria choked
too many children of her generation.

I take my life for granted and should
feel free, yet I am chained by chance
and limited by consequence,
discharge a random birthright in my blood.

Domination of White
After Wallace Stevens

In green summer,
bushes and seasoned leaves
carried the scribble of blossom
profligate with blues and reds,
purples and yellows.
But the colour of snow came creeping.
And I thought of the swan.

The swan of summer,
floating among the browns
of mud, of water, of debris,
stirring in the wanton wind
until lifted weightless
from water into gilded air.

They do not cry – swans.
Is their silence deeper against the dark
or against snow,
crystal on the wiped-out earth?

Even as green and gold were celebrating,
I saw how the snow had gathered
in clouds full of what was to be.
I saw how winter comes
creeping like the snow.
I heard the silence of the swan.

Derelict

Broken relative of those who, fully rigged,
have sail enough to venture every ocean,
to visit numerous shores, you claim only
this place where sand has locked you to the seabed
and endless waves stripped you to a skeleton.

Though men with oxygen, charts and hope, explore
for possible treasure, you keep your secrets
drowned in silence, receiving alike both shark
and dolphin, washed by the variable moon,
your frail shell forever open to the tide.

Sunlight has Tricked the Garden

Dragging out the summer, sunlight has tricked
the garden into out-of-season growth,
softened the soil where two incurable
roses lean towards the warmth and spill
their moisture back into the earth.

The apple tree, which held no fruit all year
along its unperfected branches,
now surprises, for even the frailest twigs
flash with a late springing of leaves,
green in the lingering pencilled brightness.

Yet the angle's wrong for sun to penetrate
this room, and insinuations of cold
air shuffle a pile of paper promises,
spreading them across the empty spaces.
But no-one else can close the door you opened.

Museum

The visitor

Today, here to forget familiar breakages,
I ask about the people and their gods
reaching out from the past in the potter's
etched paintings of what his fathers told.
From weathered bone and flesh, a ruined town
gathered its clay into another circling,
which a city unfinished has restored.
Wine bridges the air, returning perfume
to the grape, and oil the woman used ebbs
back to the olive, as her hands, still under mine,
hold the fired earth perfectly rounded here.

The archaeologist

Yesterday, I finished assembling the fragments
I had found travelling there and then, a woman
giving things their proper name. After all
the digging, shifting dust with brushes borrowed
from a child's box of colours, I uncovered
the random fall. Shard by shard, years of my life
were shed and fixed into the pattern's rescue.
I cannot carry oil as she once did,
for the old work and the new would each unbuild
the other. Yet those who touch this mosaic
tomorrow will not doubt that it is whole.

The woman

All day, I have waited for news of the war.
To further the smiles of my daughter, I act
the ordinary business of this house.
Between the stones, there is bread to bake,
oil to be poured, for we go on eating
and drinking toward days we may not share.
I see a messenger, bleak-faced, trudge down
the hill, and send my child to another room.
My fingers grow too cold to grasp the breaking
future, and I wonder will her mind jolt
backwards to now the moment I drop this jar?

Post-War Game

It was primaeval, that laying out
of private grief, under Pendle's
grim shadow, where once witches
drew clay portraits, pricked with thorns

the cursed part; Mother Demdike met
the devil there. The boy in silk-lined
pine would toy with war no more.
Our defence pierced his flesh, crowned

his childhood, wrote that neat full stop
above his left eye on the face's
finished page. Seeing him, I
retraced his friend's long journey

home on bleeding knees, over wild
moorland range, blasted out of all
security while, in the distance,
legendary bells dripped

ghostly notes across the high altar.
Like mortars, memories fragment.
Too young, I learned we crawl
alone through the sharpened dark.

Visit to the Psychiatric Unit

You showed me roofs from which a man might fly
and raided the toy box to magic a pattern
of lost wheels, bumpers and broken windscreens
into a silver game such as children play.

I yapped about how the British weather
had ruined a climbing holiday, the brash
behaviour of the kids in school, and rust
gradually making a scrapheap of the car.

You laid out your possessions: a painting,
yours firsthand, a book of poetry,
a nail file in a plastic case (they've let
you have it back now), and a cluttered mind.

And what did I possess? Van Gogh, secondhand
in a postcard copy, a book of trivial
stories, my nail file (that, so far, no-one
wants to take from me), and a cluttered mind.

So which of us is mad? If doctors wore white
and were labelled, if visitors had overcoats
with badges, it might be possible to guess.
Fear rises: will I need credentials to get out?

On the way home, the man in an articulated
lorry lurched without control across three lanes
whilst we skidded, stamped on screaming brakes
and waited, terrified, to see if he would make it.

But the wrenched joints clicked back in place
as he regained control then headed for some private
destination, while we moved slowly forward,
small traffic carrying too many sheets of glass.

Repairs

A homeless hooligan, this winter wind,
smashing the window into wounding spikes,
trampling down hedges grown rotten,
launching slates like missiles from the roof
to lie crazed on the flattened grass.

And day nailed to day containing
nothing but repairs to impermanent things.
Even now, in the restless night,
as we seek comfort from the fire,
a neighbour is mending a broken fence.

There's crying from a child's room
where, in the dark, a hanging
dressing-gown becomes the stuff
of nightmare. Hair sweated flat
and tears tumbling to the narrow bed.

I felt a noise, dreamt that a thief
tried to break in. I soothe with mundane
explanation till silence intervenes
like the pause between uncertain words
then, again, the sound of a hammer on wood.

Your Smile

Jaundiced eyes peer out of a sallow moon;
grey hair, streaked yellow, straggles on sterile
white pillows. You whisper *That blond young man*

loves me. Our children will be fair. Your smile
destroys seventy years building defensive
walls as your transparent fingers futilely

reach out for lost reality. *I'll give*
up my career. You have transformed all those
faded years scrubbing factory floors, as if

the mis-shapen past in her rag-bag clothes
had felt the Cinderella touch lay claim
to metamorphosis. *Are the roses*

out in my garden yet? The lonely room
that eclipsed you in some stranger's chilly
house killed even potted plants. *Has he come*

to take me home? The walls echo the wail
of sirens outside, seem to close in. *I'm*
ready, love. Surely now even stone will
mourn that you never had a golden time.

Jacket

The day's brimmed colours had smudged to grey,
the familiar moor turned hostile,
walking farther suddenly pointless.

On the way back came a glimpse of something
discarded. Off the road, where heather
stiffened the fringes of marshland,

a jacket tossed, its blackness capping
the grey; the lining still warm, yet no-one
was visible. An impossible season

for picnics, sunbathing, or sex.
Put it back, it might be needed.
But the cloth has created an itch:

An old jacket, fretted round the cuffs,
with leather patches shaped to absent elbows,
loose threads from which the buttons dangled

and, just inside the collar, a hole
edged with a few fraying fibres
where the maker's label had been torn out.

Small Boy in Irons

Tin Legs they call him at school
since a car pinioned his limbs,
strait jacketed and raised him
on a pedestal of iron feet.

He bounded out of class as if
those precisely measured cages
were just the springs that give
a Jack-in-the-box his bounce.

He tacked across the playground's slope,
wind bellying out his yellow anorak.
With the rhythm of seasons he moved,
adapting and endlessly adaptable,

then zig-zagged through the gates,
along the path and, casually mapping
his stiff-legged journey home,
splish-splashed through a trail of puddles.

Let's Face It

Already your CDs and books are packed;
they will inhabit your future. Even
your room seemed dying, its shelves
gutted and cold, while I moved forward
an hour in your life, sixty minutes
gained and lost, combining tenses.

Although you stayed a stranger here,
I still wish you genuine belonging.
But I would ask that in tailoring
your life you keep a pocket for outdated
currency, while I try to fill the gaps
with other, no doubt better, discs
and paperbacks.

                    I see now that all
you ever offered was a handkerchief,
and that not yours to give, which I resolve
to store, washed and folded, remembering
that even the hearthrug's warmth was borrowed.

The Magical Mundane

It was ordinary, the world might think,
the small pebble-dashed house, but I was free
to find adventure where I liked, often
out on the moors from daybreak to dark.
We lost ourselves in wonder, waded up rivers
to explore the source, dared rotten bridges
and flooded caves, built tunnels and dens
in snow that stayed icicle-fresh for weeks.

And over all the silver-threaded mystery
of the street names where we lived.
I imagine now those first dry moves:
council committees hunched over polished oak,
solemn men in their tight black waistcoats
fingers jabbing at maps and plans.
Did they bicker about cash and concrete,
seriously discuss the world of art,

or just grope for an equivalent
to those Paradise Rows of old?
Well, intended or not, they chose
the resounding syllables of romance:
Constable Avenue witnessed my birth
and, though I was uncertain who he was,
the word held nuances of green, depth of cloud
and the endless skies of the painter's brush.

As I walked to school with scruff-kneed friends
along the galleries of Gainsborough Rise,
my mind made tapestries of tiny homes
entwined with canvasses of painted wealth.
Between rows of grey puttied houses
all – to the overfed eye – the same,
I strolled Rossetti Avenue through Titian red,
Prussian blue, and luminous satin folds.

With mother, father, aunts, devoted dog,
I skipped among imagined elegance
through Raeburn, Romney and Reynolds Road
into the rooted sweep of heather trails.
We scuffed our shoes, fell off our bikes,
chalked our own rainbow art on whipping tops,
jumped square to square to avoid the cracks
on pavements of Hogarth and Creswick and Orpen.

Then – the place I kept for special days:
without family, friends, or toys, just me
alone with the words in my head. I wandered
the sepia street but in truth I travelled
through rose-marble glow, breathed honeyed
bloom, gazed at the gold-topped waves
of Mediterranean blue, enthralled
by the magical mundane of Alma-Tadema Grove.

Fire and Ice in Cambridge

King's College by the log fire
in the maple panelled room.
I watched the snow outside drift
thick, untrammelled, and quiet.

Inside, music reached for us,
not so much heard as tasted,
breathed, and spread throughout the blood
of this golden group of friends.

Then I had to leave alone
and face the cold; so now when
I linger outside the glass
Brahms once more shivers through me

with the things that might have been.

When the Time has Come

I
When the time has come, you can tell. The sheep,
on edge but tired, droop at first on folded
limbs but soon haul restless bodies up
to stand on legs that look too frail to lift
the swollen bellies, then awkwardly kneel
and nibble grass. No posture gives them ease.

Until, like flung waves furling on the shore,
the ewe sends ripples from her shoulders down
to push out a flurry of limbs and sprawl.
She licks the lamb's coat clean then nudges him
to stand up ready to run from danger
if the creak of black wings breaks the air.

The lamb must learn to walk at once. He wobbles
on thin wavy legs then staggers, crumples,
stands, collapses but, finally, he nuzzles
milk and the ritual can begin again.
Everything seems easier now and with a slither
of watery membrane the twin slides to earth.

II
Today, the metal grip of winter lingers
in the field where a ewe circles and twists
over and over but, when the struggle brings
a lamb, she doesn't even look at it. Her flesh
troubles her and the newborn is ignored.
Without her help, very soon he will die.

Now the ewe contorts from shoulder to tail,
shoulder to tail, but nothing happens.
She lies inert then walks, crouches, heaves.
A sudden tiny head appears. The twin's amazed
by this exciting world but, trapped inside,
can only turn eager eyes from left to right.

The owner's far from here: this townie must act.
A young lad's found whose father farmed here once
until foot and mouth wiped out his flock.
The ewe lurches away, won't let the boy near.
He holds the fading firstborn and, even now,
the ewe's deep history means she must come back.

Memories of what his father did have stayed
with the boy. He pushes the head back in,
probes to find and turn a shoulder. And then –
beating against the dark – the second lamb slips free.
The sun breaks out from behind the grey
as both life and the late spring begin.

Burned

There is now a reaching of the whole flesh
as if not just the injured hand but all
the body gathers here to hide the pus,
a prissy lady trying to pull lace
across the windows of a private mess.

Ironic, to have studied fire precautions,
made up a cardboard cover strong enough
to foil the flame and mastered the routine
for every casual rehearsal date
then, when it really mattered, to forget.

One looks for signs: words that couldn't be said,
the gun that jammed and had to be fired twice;
a holding back we should have parodied.
So, all I have left on the balance sheet
is a red scar; that, and your bloodstained shirt.

White Ovver

White ovver int Yorksher Dales.
After freezin fog comes
snow-crumb, rime frost icin
that magics what wer clarty folds
inter this filigree wonderland:

sparklin hillsides wi sheer scars
o trampled shell n skeleton
an plateaus o rough an weathered rock,
Dales limestone pavements,
grit dahn to tbone.

These pavements wer born o scourin ice,
a mosaic o corrugate, ankle-brekkin
clints n grykes, constantly carved
bi weatherin as snowmelt
seeps inter tpotholes n caves.

Int deep narrer grykes, grow sturdy Hawthorns
honed inter craggy live sculpture
bi tchill n fettlin wind; along wi Bloody
Cranesbill, precious Baneberry,
rare Rigid Buckler, an Limestone Fern.

Dahlias, Fuchsias, Camellias,
tremulous warmth-only blooms,
nay, thas all of yer nobbut offcumdens:
so doant think to come ere
wi yer fancy ways.

To a Friend Losing Her Sight

Crowding your eyes, this pain only
limits physical light. Stored noons
stay vivid even where pressure
has splintered clarity, flooded
regions where sight and insight meet.

Pretending dark, I try to share
that blackness behind the screen,
but closing lids is a makeshift
trick the mind throws out, filling
the blanks with pictures of the past:

Road signs we both misread, talking
of lines that don't appear on maps;
other drivers' v-signs when we stalled;
red faces mouthing as we swerved
hampered by a foggy windscreen.

It seems absurd that now you wait
for strangers to enlarge your vision,
although it is perhaps appropriate
for one without self-pity that
others should drain the tears from you.

Whatever the doctors say, I risk
this forecast: you will go on seeing,
handling blind spots gamely and, because
feeling guides you, only put your
finger on constructive syllables.

Literary Weekend

A buttoned-up beginning,
showing off Sunday-best selves.
Clutching luggage safely locked,
we spoke only of missed trains,
cancelled buses, cups of tea.

Loosening came bit by bit,
unparcelled a slanging match.
Someone threw-up in the loo
then, sickened by her own sex,
threw in her lot with the men.

We fumbled with fastenings,
began to appear without
make-up, sloppy in shapeless
dressing-gowns. Lotharios
preferred to flash pyjamas.

Narratives unfolded, brought
confessions, entanglements,
even a squabble over
stray kittens. Some blabbed in drink
and some in desperation.

One poet, giving himself
away, line by line unwound
the common threads of nightmare,
uncovered old scars, and stripped
away our shifty layers.

Minds unsettled by home truths
grew mussed up as slept-in clothes.
Finished, I packed my crumpled,
worn belongings and wondered
what was left salvageable.

Pistol

The stock curls exactly
into the palm's folds,
cushioned by head, heart
and life-lines, fitting
the hand without discomfort,
and with too much normality
extends the human frame.

Clench to a fist, trigger
the barrel's gambling drum,
and the one inflexible finger
clouds the air with grey.

Made to start a race
or end it, now charged
with blanks, exploding through
each rehearsal, it points the play
forward to the final act.

Love Poem – a Prisoner's Request

Will you bring me a love poem? -
To send to the wife.
I took in the great poets -
resonant, subtle, crafted verse.

No. No. And, no.
What is it you're asking for?
A love poem.

But, they're the best there is.
They aren't love poems for my wife.

Ah, you want me to ...
Yes.
(And, he'll pretend he wrote it).
Please.

So, I wrote a love poem
to another woman, as if I was a man,
a man who doesn't like anything *poncy,*
arty-farty, middle-fucking-class.

I stayed up night after night, crossed out
image and symbol, ditched words with rich connotations.
It was bloody, fucking difficult.

I didn't keep a copy but, even if I had,
I wouldn't let anyone read it because
he loved it and he sent it and it's hers.

All I can say is, it possibly wavered toward the trite,
but might be the most worthwhile poem I'll ever write.

How Far Will You Go?

Down to bare rock?
To the whirlpool that kills, or liberates?

The journey is both razorblade and velvet
and these devouring waves can drown
any perception of a world
every second being re-made.

If the biting coral doesn't pierce your flesh
maybe you'd better scrape the skin yourself
and allow a rawness, an openness to risk.

You can stay inshore
of the Great Barrier Reef
or you can dare the open sea.

Inside

Haiku approved by the men on D Wing

Why am I looking
outward now from this window?
   I can see nothing.

For My Today Girls of Tomorrow

For you I would have kept a hoard
of green, washed by the breeze, webbed by birds,
but will you even hold
wilderness, dig your fingers in earth?
I would have gifted crag and river, but wasted
your certain rock, lost
the dependable moon and tide,
and have very little in my fist.

But such lines won't do. You'd shrug at winged metaphor.
We don't even use the same language and
so, risking the knife-edge of modern scorn,
I hold out what's left in my open hand:

4u 2day grls ov 2moro i leve
amng the sht n dbris tht obdr8 wrd lv.